IMAGES OF ENGLAND

AROUND
WHITEHAVEN
THE SECOND SELECTION

CW00952516

Marchon Products Ltd, seen here in 1955, became a major producer of sulphuric acid. A subsidiary company, Solway Chemicals, was set up to handle the production process and this called for a huge quantity of the principal raw material – anhydrite. This too was mined on site and relied heavily on the shot-firers' skill to win the mineral.

IMAGES OF ENGLAND

AROUND
WHITEHAVEN
THE SECOND SELECTION

ALAN W. ROUTLEDGE

The
History
Press

First published in 2001 by Tempus Publishing

Reprinted in 2010 by
The History Press
The Mill, Brimscombe Port,
Stroud, Gloucestershire, GL5 2QG
www.thehistorypress.co.uk

ISBN 978 0 7524 2239 8

Typesetting and origination by
Tempus Publishing Limited
Printed and bound in Great Britain by
Marston Book Services Limited, Didcot

Increasing levels of business by bigger and bigger vessels, coupled with the fact that Whitehaven
was a tidal harbour, made the use of dredgers absolutely essential to the efficient working of the
port. Over the years there have been a number of dredgers employed in this vital service and
this one, in use in 1905, was of the bucket elevator type.

Contents

Acknowledgements

My thanks for allowing the use of images and photographs from their collections must go to The Beacon, Whitehaven; Albright & Wilson Ltd; Mr Jimmy O'Neil; and especially to the late Billy Phillips, who so kindly donated several original glass plates from the 1930s, some of which are shown for the first time in this volume. I am also indebted to my friends for their encouragement, especially Ray Devlin, Bob McConnell and Michael Moon.

Parton around 1910 was a much busier place than it is today. The railway sidings have gone as have many of the buildings in the village. In the background the harbour piers at Whitehaven can be clearly seen.

Introduction

Almost all the photographs used in this compilation have been drawn from a number of private or institutional picture collections. That these images are still in existence today is due to some very careful and time-consuming work on the part of the various collectors. The title *Around Whitehaven* is not born of accident but because the book contains photographs taken in the outlying villages of St Bees, Kells, Sandwith and Parton and some areas closer to the town centre, including the Ginns, the New and Old Towns, the town centre and the Harbour. The dates of the photographs range from the 1850s to the late 1960s and include some prints made from a number of glass negatives found in the roof of an old photographers' studio and which were in their original boxes dated 1929 and 1930.

The book has been laid out in the form of a photographic journey starting in St Bees, in the south, and ending at Parton, in the north. On this perambulation we also take a look at the industrial make-up of the Preston Isle, particularly its chemical manufacture and coal mining industries. From Kells our path takes us through the Ginns and Preston Street to the South Harbour. Leaving the South Harbour at Lowther Street we travel to the Corkickle Brewery before returning to the North Harbour by way of Whitehaven's many varied and interesting streets. On route we stop off at The Theatre Royal, The Howgill Street Infirmary, the Playground and the Trinity National or Central School. Leaving the North Harbour, local transport comes under the spotlight before the final visit to Parton.

The choice of this particular route was not an easy one to make and was, in part, a response to many an observation made by friends and acquaintances referring to the lack of pictures of the villages in other similar books. There are now over a dozen books of photographs of Whitehaven, but almost all concentrate on the town centre itself. In this volume an attempt has been made to redress that balance, but in a volume of this size it is impossible to cover all those outlying towns and villages. To the folk of Egremont, Hensingham, Cleator and Cleator Moor all that can be said is 'maybe next time'.

Finally I dedicate the book to Frances, my wife, for all her understanding over the past forty-five years.

Alan W Routledge
March 2001

In their book, Harry Fancy and Ray Devlin tell us that William Pit was *the most dangerous mine in the kingdom*. Such a claim is not without justification as there were several hundred men and boys killed throughout the working life of the colliery. By 1910 all the miners carried safety lamps both for visibility down the mine and for testing for methane gas – a constant threat to life and limb. Note also that these men and boys outside William Pit lamp-house are wearing just simple caps and not the hard miners' helmet of recent years.

One

St Bees and the Preston Isle

Whitehaven stands at the northern end of the St Bees valley and originally consisted of just a handful of agricultural workers' and fishermen's cottages. The residents served the needs of the monks of St Bees Priory, providing them with horses, cattle, pigs, barley, fish, coal and salt. The Priory was founded in 1125 by William Meschin, although there is some evidence of an earlier church on the site dating back to Saxon times. St Bees valley is divided roughly down the middle by the Poe (now Pow) Beck which flows into the Irish Sea both at Whitehaven in the north and St Bees in the south and in doing so forms an island on the western side. This is the Preston Isle which rises steeply some 300ft from the valley floor and even more spectacularly on the seaward side. The Preston Isle was the location of the Howgill Colliery, the collective name for many of Whitehaven's coal pits, including Croft, Ladysmith, Kells, Raven Hill, Haig, Thwaite, King and Saltom, the latter being the first coal mine to be worked entirely under the sea. In this chapter we journey from St Bees to the very outskirts of Whitehaven following the coastal way.

ST. BEES, MAIN STREET SHOWING POST OFFICE, CUMBERLAND.   N° 178

The village of St Bees, c. 1910. It lies along the main road to Egremont and Nethertown. There were several small businesses on Main Street together with at least four inns or hotels. These included the Albert Hotel, the Blacksmith's Arms, the Oddfellows' Inn and the Queen's Hotel; all of these properties are still in use today.

Looking north along Main Street towards Whitehaven in 1890. The buildings of Lady Farm are on the right while the farmhouse itself is on the left. For many years Lady Farm was in the hands of the Clark family who in more recent times were great supporters of the Wyndham Pony Club and St Bees Annual Show.

The fine old Maypole tradition has long gone from the village diary, although St Bees now holds an annual fair with such events as a pram race around the village pubs. The old procession used to pass the railway station and Grindal House. For many years the house has been part of St Bees Grammar School, which was founded in April 1583 by the Archbishop of Canterbury, Edmund Grindal.

The men and boys of Whitehaven found much pleasure in simple things in the 1920s. With many people out of work and having little or no money, sailing hand-made boats with their friends at St Bees after a three-mile walk was an enjoyable escape from the troubles of the times.

Although three miles or so from the centre of Whitehaven, people walked to St Bees, almost as a matter of course, for a paddle on the beach or to play all manner of games on the sands and dunes. A trip to St Bees was often the ultimate destination for the much appreciated Sunday School outing, which children looked forward to for weeks beforehand.

St Bees was justly proud of its beach; the wide expanse of clean sands attracted both the visitor and local alike. Many holidaymakers chose to stay at the Sea Cote Hotel, which was close to the beach and to the golf course. In the 1920s several of these larger terraced houses also served as bed and breakfast stopovers.

Just a few yards from the hotel were these good views of the beach, as well as the sand dunes, which protected it from any cold easterly breezes. The small hut sold tea and hot water (for people to make their own tea) to many a thirsty bather in 1920. Now it is a beach shop and café and the central dunes have given way to a neat promenade.

Leaving St Bees by the cliff footpath
affords a final look back at the Sea
Cote and the beach stretching away
to Coulderton in the distance. Well
before this image was made in 1932,
local builders carted shingle off the
beach for building foundation work
and many a garden was decorated
with an edge of small beach stones.
Crossing over Tomlin (sometimes
called the South Head), the path
falls steeply into the delightfully
secluded Fleswick Bay. Getting into
and out of Fleswck is not for the
short of wind, but for those who
do make the trip, the rewards are
worth it. The bay was as quiet a
place in 1929 as it is today (except
for the Wainwright Coast to Coast
walkers). The beach was at one
time of considerable interest to
makers of jewellery; semi-precious
stones were to be found in
abundance on the shore. The North
Head houses the RSPB's St Bees
reserve which has some exciting
viewing platforms providing
views of the nest sites of fulmars,
razorbills, guillemots, kittiwakes,
puffins and herring gulls.

At the top of the North Head stands the St Bees Lighthouse and this postcard from 1927 shows both the lighthouse and the keeper's cottages. The light was fully manned until just a few years ago, but now both the lighthouse and the fog warning hooters are automated and the cottages let to non-Trinity House residents.

The private road from the lighthouse falls steeply down to the village of Sandwith. The village has changed little in outward appearance since 1907, the date of this picture, except that some properties have been modernized. The village had three inns – the Dog and Partridge, the White Horse and the Lowther Arms. The latter two have since been combined into one business.

North of Sandwith and within the Parish of St Peter's lies the village of Kells. Kells grew around some of the earliest coal mines to be worked in the Whitehaven Colliery, including Kells, King, Thwaite, Saltom, and Raven Hill pits. Throughout the 1920s Whitehaven Borough Council built hundreds of council houses to rehouse people from the older parts of the town and an old Army hut was erected and consecrated by the Bishop of Barrow-in-Furness for the use of the local Anglican community. The foundation stone for a permanent church was laid by the Bishop of Carlisle in 1938 and the new St Peter's, seen here under construction, cost £10,000 and was consecrated by the Bishop on 6 September 1939 – just three days after the start of the Second World War.

During the summer of 1914 open-air services were held by the Primitive Methodist community around Kells and, as a direct result, a small church group was formed which held its meetings in local houses. Later they met in yet another old Army hut known as 'Sandy's Mission'. This was replaced in 1921 by a new chapel and even in 1971 it remained an imposing structure.

Directly across the road was Kells Miners' Welfare and Community Centre, home to many leisure facilities including a fine bowling green. In 1941 the bowling team were winners of the Whitehaven League.

Saltom Pit was one of the first coal mines to have its entire workings underneath the sea. Sunk in 1729, production had long ceased by 1905 when this picture was taken. After the pit closed, the shaft was used as a methane vent from the other pits still left working in the area.

Once mining activity had come to an end, the beach became very popular with local people. At weekends, during school holidays and on warm summer evenings, this little bay was a playground for many a family. This view shows that the summer of 1925 was no exception. The beach remained popular until quite recently, when subsidence caused the path to disintegrate.

Basket Road was home to many mining families and there was always a great sense of community. This can not be better typified than by this children's Coronation party. From left to right, back row: Mrs McCartney, Evelyn Hinde, Agnes George, Mrs Tolson, Betty and Margaret Bulman. Middle row: -?-, Lizzie Holmes, Mrs Mullholland, Mrs Lennox, Maimme Brannon, Dick Swailes, Kath Ward, Mrs Woods. Front row: Pat Rooney, Maureen Tembey, Mary Brannon, Mary Mullholland.

Many children from Kells, Woodhouse and the Ginns spent their early school days at Monkwray Junior School. The top class of 1946/47 poses here for the annual school photograph. From left to right, back row: Billy Franks, Frank Acton, Charlie Morton, David Mawson, Dennis Graham, Derrick Chorley, Edwin McAlone, Jim Storey, Tom Pullin, Ronnie Hoy, Victor Parry, Eddie Aitkin. Middle row: Harry Callow, Joan Henderson, Betty Madine, Mona Short, Sally Nicholson, Chrissie Baxter, Jean Billington, Maureen Shepherd, -?-, Audrey Mccartney, Dick Sim, James Radcliffe. Front row: -?-, -?-, Jean Cartmell, Mary Hardie, Elsie Smith, Mabel Telford, Sheila Bawden, Harriet Lewthwaite, Audrey Hiddleston, Mary Atkinson, Eileen Jones, Pat Doran and Jean Jones. Sitting: Tom Scott, Henry McQuire, Frank Snow, George Walker, Stanley Kellett.

Two

The Industrial Scene:
Kells and the Preston Isle

The Preston Isle was the location for many early industrial ventures which included chemicals and mining at Kells; glass and pottery manufacture at the Ginns; brick-making near the Low Road; and a good number of farms in the outlying district. Over the next few pages images of mining at the Haig Colliery and chemical production at the Ladysmith Works of Marchon Products Ltd are examined. When it ceased production in January 1986, Haig was already the last deep coal mine in Cumbria and naturally its closure brought coal mining in the traditional manner to an end. Ladysmith Pit was abandoned as a coal production facility in 1931 with only the washery buildings remaining in use for Haig coal. However in 1943 Marchon Products Ltd moved into the unused pit-top premises to start what was to grow into one of the greatest chemical works in Europe. Much has happened to these industries since the heady days of the 1960s when Haig employed over 1,600 mine workers and Marchon employed no fewer than 3,500 people on the site.

Marchon Products had already begun its rapid expansion by 1953 when the first of its phosphoric acid plants was under construction. Standing in the foreground is Preston Howes Farm on whose land much of the factory was built.

On 6 December 1939, Frank Schon and Fred Marzillier occupied offices in London, following their flight from the Nazi occupation of their home countries, and registered a new company, Marchon Products Ltd. Shattered when their London premises were bombed in the Blitz, they moved north to Whitehaven and after using a number of small warehouses around the town in 1943 they settled in the old Ladysmith Pit and Tar Works, where they began the manufacture of firelighters from a mixture of sawdust, old fat and naphthalene. Mixing was crude by today's standards and packing was by hand. In these early photographs a young process worker (thought to be Joe Bennett) is feeding the mix into moulds which produced a bar rather like a large chocolate block. Hilda Denwood (foreground) and her colleagues are packing the firelighters for sale.

One problem that was to continually dog the company in its development was isolation from both its potential customers and from its source of raw materials. In an effort to counteract this, the company built its own fatty alcohol plant in 1955 and this photograph from 1956 shows a tanker outside the distillation unit.

One of the main reasons for the success of the company was the quality of the sales team, who not only covered the UK but jetted off all over the world. By 1965 the sales effort was divided into several business units, of which Detergents and Toiletries was one. Clockwise from the left: Otto Secher (sales director), Mike Dufaye (managing director Marchon France), George W. Pekarek (sales manager, later director), -?-, Col. R.D. Cribb (sales manager, sulphuric acid), Alan Telford (London office manager), Jim McMenemy (sales manager, detergent phosphates), John M. Bromley (technical sales manager), -?-, Albert Taylor (technical director).

This superb image from 1970 shows the back side of the works with the one remaining Ladysmith Pit building still in use, in the foreground. It housed several of the company's development units under the management of Bob Southward. Immediately behind are the

phosphoric acid storage tanks and railway sidings. In the distance the steaming stacks vent water vapour from the phosphate dryers and tripolyphosphate kilns.

A work force of 3,000 needed feeding, particularly when working unsociable hours, and the factory's several canteens had a high reputation. The works canteen was used for many a celebration and in 1975 a buffet was prepared to commemorate the presentation of a third

Following a great deal of discussion Marchon Products Ltd agreed to sell the technical know-how for the production of fatty alcohol to the USSR and in 1963 the a plant was commissioned at Volgodonsk. During the earlier part of the year Russian plant managers were trained at Whitehaven. From left to right: Alan W. Routledge (training organizer), V.P. Tyagoon, Madame Kostikova, L. Shevchenko, G. Friedberg, N.N. Kostikov.

Queen's Award to Industry to the company. The ladies surrounding Bert (Shiggy) Ratcliffe include Madge Kitchen, Doris Farrer, Madge Skinner, Rose Tranmere, Margaret Kellett, Mrs Groggin, and Mrs McCourt.

When Albright & Wilson Ltd took over Marchon Products Ltd in 1955 Fred Marzillier left the company and Frank Schon continued in his role as managing director at Whitehaven and also as a main board director at A&W. Councillor Fred Baxter, Mayor, presented both founders with the Freedom of Whitehaven at a ceremony in 1961.

A serious shortage of sulphur during the Korean War in 1951 had a damaging effect on the manufacture and supply of sulphuric acid. As a major user of this basic chemical, Marchon had to look to alternate sources for the acid. Unknown to the company, it was sitting on a vast deposit of anhydrite, which could be used to make SO_2, the main requirement for the sulphuric acid process, and in doing so it was also to provide a very useful by-product – cement. In the middle of 1955 the first two kilns came on stream yielding some 200,000 tons of acid and a similar quantity of cement per year. In 1962 a further kiln was commissioned which increased the capacity of both acid and cement by 70,000 tons and in 1967 kilns 4 and 5 further increased capacity to a total of 450,000 tons of sulphuric acid and the same of cement – making the site one of the largest manufacturers of these vital raw materials in the world.

Mining anhydrite was a very different proposition than extracting coal and this was true from the very start of operations. The vast anhydrite deposits which lay under St Bees Head were reached by means of a long drift and the mine was opened on 11 January 1955 by Sir Robert Chance, Lord Lieutenant of Cumberland. The sinking of this drift and the building of the first two kilns and acid plant cost some £3 million. Getting at the coal which lay under the sea was achieved, at Haig, by means of a 900ft vertical shaft which was started in 1914 but the first commerical coal production did not occur until 1920. Unlike the very hard anhydrite measures, the coal field had many geological faults and was gassy – a constant source of danger which in the end cost many lives.

Over the period 1920 to 1986, Haig Colliery became the most important coal-winning facility in the Cumbrian coal field. As other pits were closed Haig absorbed many of the miners who had lost their jobs, but in 1928 it was just one of four in Whitehaven. Note the lack of surface buildings and the brick-built ventilation air lock around No. 5 shaft.

The winter of 1966 gave a spectacular view from the top of No. 5 headgear. Looking north No. 4 fills the foreground, with the old boiler house cooling ponds just behind. On the skyline is Basket Road, which was home to many miners.

Safety was always the watchword in the mining industry and regular maintenance was the key to a safe working environment. This meant changing the shear wheels from time to time and renewing the winding rope at regular intervals. Every few months the ropes were shortened to allow for the stretch which occurred under heavy load.

Coal was moved from the washeries to the break top by steam powered shunting engines such as *Repulse* and *Weasel*. Colliery waste had also to be moved to the tip and this too was done by steam engines. This photograph shows a side tipping wagon about to be taken to the bank.

The steam shunting engines were an essential part of the pit's ability to work efficiently and their crews played no small part in the safe running of the transport system. The Haig site needed several engines for smooth running. This is the *Weasel*'s crew in 1960. From left to right: Nelson Johnstone, Bobby Southward, Allan Smith, Tommy Haston.

Getting coal to the hurries on the harbour-side was always something of a problem; the steep drop down the cliff face taxed mining engineers over many years. In the 1960s coal wagons were lowered to the harbour by means of rope haulage, which operated on a counterweight system where two full wagons going down would pull two empties up the incline.

During the life of the pit the miners were its lifeblood and strength. They made the colliery tick! Miners worked some of the most demanding shift systems used in modern industry. The normal shift was eight hours underground in the dark and it was a relief to get back to the surface, safe and sound. From left to right: Les Vernon, R Brannon, -?-, Billy Batey, Jim 'Wacko' Kitchen.

During 1975 and 1976, as part of an extensive coal development plan by the National Coal Board, some £2 million was spent on improved surface facilities at Haig Colliery. The old Ladysmith washery was abandoned and replaced with this new one at Haig which opened in October 1976. Unfortunately this major development could not, in the end, save the pit from closure.

The normal manner in which the miners entered and left the pit was by the No. 4 shaft, and in order to know who was underground a system of tallies or discs was used. Before going below the men were issued with their personal disc which on their return was handed to the tally man. From left to right: Russell Lofthouse, -?-, Richard Percival, Ken Hodgson, Eddie Bowman, -?-, Jimmy Powe.

The last shift to go down Haig colliery was the night shift of the 26 January 1986. Just a few hours after this photograph was taken the pit closed for good. The cages were cut and allowed to fall to the bottom of the shafts which were immediately filled in. Thus ended all deep coal mining in the Cumberland Coal Field.

Three

The Ginns to South Harbour

The oldest parts of Whitehaven were on the west bank of the Poe Beck and thus, in a sense, still on the Preston Isle. Early street rental books tended to lump several streets together as the Old Town and these included the Market Place, Swing Pump Lane, Quay Street, the West Strand and the host of alleyways and lanes which dissected the area. As the town grew and industries developed, the Ginns, Preston Street, the New Town and the New Houses were built. The Ginns took its name from the horse-drawn pumps which kept the coal mines clear of water; the area was settled by coal miners so that they could be close to their place of work. Later other industries sprang up around the Ginns, especially glass-making and pottery manufacture. Copras was also made from scrap iron, and sulphuric acid or vitriol as it was called was produced from iron pyrites found in conjunction with coal. From the Lowthers' point of view, all of these industries were just what the doctor ordered because they required great quantities of coal, something which led to their being located as near to the mines as possible.

Running from the Coach Road to the Glass House School, Bentinck Road is the only part of the Ginns left standing and in use today. The road is seen here in 1965 and not much has changed over the intervening years.

While all around was falling into decay and dereliction in 1954, the Lowther Arms remained occupied and open for business. However the day of the bulldozer came and it too was swept away!

How many people can remember Echo margarine on sale at 8d per half-pound block? With butter in short supply, even if not still on ration, in 1954, margarine was the only alternative even though it was rock hard and definitely did not taste like butter! M.T. Blight's corner shop was a popular place to buy food, sweets and the daily newspaper.

The Glass House was originally set up for the manufacture of bottles for use in the export of strong ales to the Colonies, but the venture soon failed and the property became a school. The Glass House School eventually moved into new premises on Monkwray Brow and the old glass works became the Colliery Mission. Their 'Band of Hope' is pictured outside the building in 1905.

The New Houses were built in 1788 to house mine workers, thereby giving the Lowther family an edge over their competition. The residents formed a close-knit community and a birthday was cause for communal celebration here in 1925.

Looking north, Preston Street led from the Ginns to the New Town and consisted of several good dwelling houses and a couple of pubs on the western side and the Whitehaven Auction Mart and the railway goods yard on the other side. The photograph above dates from the 1960s and was taken shortly before the demolition of the Fox and Hounds Inn. This popular pub was previously known as the Dog and the Greyhound. Across the road, the goods yard was home to several businesses, including F. Watson & Co. They were principally coal, coke and lime merchants as well as being available for carting and furniture removal. Seen directly behind the Watson wagons in 1901 are Knowles and Fiddlers, animal feed merchants. Further to the left are some of the chimney tops of the New Houses.

Preston Street opens out into the New Town which, although it may have been new at one time, is one of the oldest parts of the town and was the location of several clay pipe works, giving rise to street names such as Pipehouse Lane. Nos 62 to 70 New Town were typical of the workers' cottages of the time and many similar dwellings could be found anywhere in town. A little nearer the town centre stood The Victoria Vaults, an inn which had a good trade and which changed its name to the Victoria soon after she came to the throne. Rather like the Lowther Arms in the Ginns, it remained in business until all of the surrounding properties had been pulled down by the breakers' men. Both photographs date from 1958. Not far from the Victoria Vaults stood one of Whitehaven's many engineering works, the Newtown Foundry.

At the end of the short lane between the Old and New Towns stands the Dusty Miller Inn and this too is a public house around which the adjoining buildings have since been demolished. Nevertheless, the 'Dusty' still remains popular today. The Old Town, pictured here in 1956, has become part of Whitehaven's inner ring road.

The Albion Street Bakery was owned and operated by Mr G. Anderson in 1905, who obviously delivered the freshly baked bread about the town by horse and cart. It seems the horse was partial to the odd loaf too!

Swing Pump Lane runs parallel to the Market Place; indeed many of the Market shops back onto the lane. The visitor would find great difficulty in finding the lane today, as it has now been widened as part of the ring road system. Only the backs of the shops remain and these have been tidied up and have a suitably wide pavement. The opposite side is bounded by the multi-storey car park and other business ventures. Until the road was widened the whole area was criss-crossed with small lanes of which Littledale Lane was typical. Leading up to The Mount and the Ranters Chapel, the lane was named after William Littledale one of the family of merchants involved in trade with the colonies and the West Indies. Indeed many of the town's streets and lanes were called after other great merchant families.

The Hogarth Mission was finally demolished in the 1960s, making way for a new canteen for the Crosthwaite Memorial School. This was perhaps a fitting end for the mission as the school was church-maintained. The chapel had something of a chequered history, having been in turn an Anglican, a Methodist and a Primitive Methodist chapel and even a candle factory.

Tucked onto the end of the mission were two small houses, together known as Hogarth House. Situated at the junction of The Mount and Rosemary Lane, both heavily populated areas, the property was ideally placed for a shop. The ground floor window had been modified to serve as a shop window. By 1958 the chapel and the house were in line for early demolition.

Following a report to the council by Dr John Hopkinson FRS, this handsome brick building was converted for the production of electrical power in 1892. The new generating plant cost £28,000 to complete and on 1 September 1893, 450 electric lights lit up the streets of the town for the first time. The generators produced direct current which was used exclusively in the town centre, with the outlying districts drawing their needs from the alternating current supplies of the National Grid. In 1948 all electricity supplies were nationalized. Generating in Whitehaven ceased and the power station became little more than a substation. Soon after 1956 the area was cleared of all residual slum and derelict buildings but it was not until 1996 that the old power station was restored for use as a sewerage pumping plant and the mount steps were attractively restored.

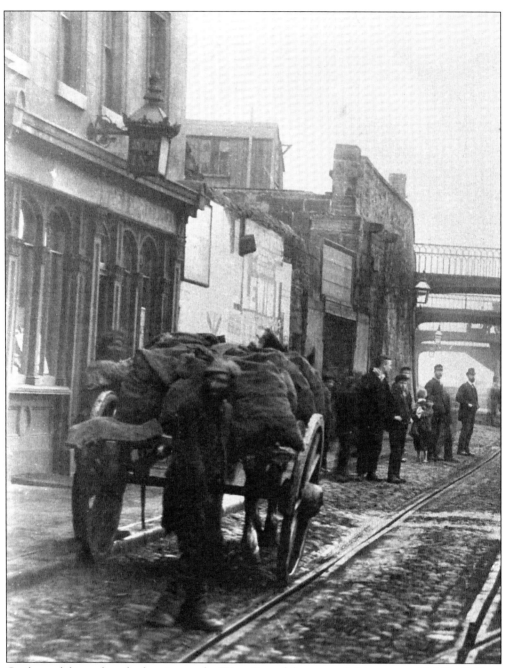

Coal was delivered to the hurries on the West Strand for onward shipment to Dublin, Belfast, Douglas and Ramsey. Loading coal was dirty and thirsty work for the coal layers; the latter problem could be assuaged by a quick visit to any one of three pubs which stood wall to wall besides the hurries. One of them was the Blue Anchor, pictured here in 1895. Of the three, the first to close after referral to the Compensation Board in Carlisle was the Blacksmith's Arms and the last was the Lighthouse Inn.

Quay Street connects the Market Place and the West Strand. It originally ran at a different angle from that of today and was once described as 'the dirtiest street in Britain, save for Lace Street in Liverpool'. From the end of the Second World War until its closure, soon after this image was made in 1955, The Braddylls Arms had one of the best darts teams in town.

The West Strand stood waiting for the demolition men in 1956 and all the property to the right of the Royal Standard has now long gone. Indeed the site of the nearer building forms part of the greatly widened junction with Quay Street leading directly onto the Sugar Tongue which has recently been restored to some of its former glory.

Dobson and Musgrave Ltd (wholesale grocers and provisions merchants) and The Ship Inn used to stand on the West Strand. Pictured here in 1960, Dobson and Musgrave moved their business to the Barracks Mill in Catherine Street where they traded for a few more years. In the years between the wars just to walk past the open doors of the warehouse was a treat for the senses – the smell of well-cured bacon and ham, tea, freshly ground coffee, biscuits and spices must have seemed like heaven to the hungry lad. To day the building has been converted to flats with a great view of the Harbour. Meanwhile the Ship Inn, seen below around 1933, fell to the bulldozer when Quay Street was widened. Note the suit, trilby hat, bow tie and gold watch chain, all of which suggest Sunday best.

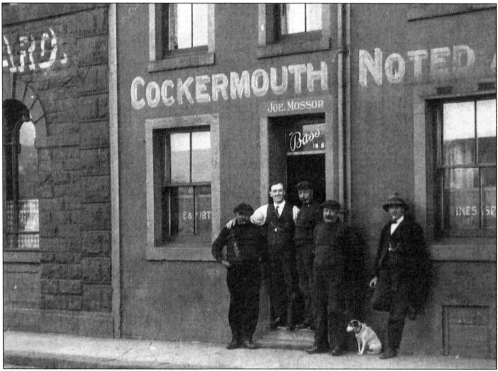

Four
The South Harbour

The South Harbour was without doubt the oldest and the busiest part of the dock system. It was here on the south side of the creek that Christopher Lowther chose to build the Old Quay in 1634. Shorter than it is today, it nevertheless provided considerable shelter to the collier vessels loading at the hurries. The great influx of merchants, who came to Whitehaven as a direct result of these harbour improvements, led to an unprecedented growth in trade with the Baltic States, the Colonies, mainland Europe, Ireland and the West Indies. This in turn led to the building of first the Merchants' Quay or Sugar Tongue and later of the Lime Tongue. Passenger vessels sailed daily to Dublin, Glasgow and Liverpool and it was possible to embark for many foreign ports on a regular basis. Whitehaven's transatlantic trade lifted the standing of the port to the third most important in the kingdom, whilst the coal exports to Ireland made Whitehaven the second busiest port in the land after London. There was however, a price to pay for having much of the town's commerce in just one or two baskets. The loss of the American War of Independence badly effected the tobacco trade, which was thereafter all but lost, and without that trade, the prosperity of Whitehaven suffered to an extent from which it never fully recovered.

With the passage of time even the coal trade began to be uneconomic, throwing families out of work from time to time. There was no dole or income support to be had and in the 1920s people had to scratch a living as best they could. Here an old lady gathers coal from the dockside railway line. This was illegal and if she was caught, a fine or even jail was the likely outcome.

Even when funds were short in the 1880s a good crowd could always be expected at the annual regatta. Held in the harbour there were all manner of fun events in addition to the more serious racing of fishing boats. Coal layers rowed using their giant shovels as oars and there was always the local ham at the end of the greasy pole.

As a general rule, after a successful launch, boats were towed from the shipyards round to the Sugar Tongue for fitting out. The *Thirlmere* (1711 tons) was one such vessel, seen here being fitted out and prepared for her maiden voyage in 1874.

Even as late as 1904 coal was still being loaded onto collier vessels at the Hurries on the West Strand. The buildings on the end of the Old Quay have long been demolished but in their time they included a bath house using salt water drawn from the sea.

Local photographer Belman used his skill to capture this fine image of the Sugar Tongue in 1904 with several local fishing smacks unloading their catches. It was here that the trawlers took on ice and salt for their next trip to the fishing grounds. The coaster is probably the *Busk*.

The Custom House Dock was full of activity in 1905 with fishing boats often stacked three and four deep along the side of the Sugar Tongue, a sight often repeated over the next ninety years. Even then the slipway was used by a few small pleasure craft.

A small collier vessel is moored at the Old Quay as she waits her turn to load at the Hurries in 1904. The harbour was cleared of silt by regular dredging and the forerunner to the *Clearway* can be seen at work. In the seventeenth and eighteenth centuries this work was carried out at low tide by bucket and shovel with the mud and gravel carried away by horse and cart!

When the herring and mackerel were running as they were in 1910, the harbour often filled up with fishing boats from all over the north of Britain as they followed the shoals of fish through the Irish Sea.

One of Whitehaven's favourite characters was Barney the goose who could be seen anywhere about town. Everybody fed him and were rewarded by his antics. It seems, in 1910, he could even stop a train whilst attracting a crowd. Barney certainly knew how to earn his daily bread and took his name from his breed – a barnacle goose.

An attractive assortment of brigs tied up at the Sugar Tongue was a familiar sight in 1880 where they unloaded their mixed cargoes from all parts of the world. Here, too, they loaded up with manufactured goods destined for some exotic port at the end of their outward journey. The harbour gave good protection from the elements which could be inclement at times.

H.M. Submarine H.50 steams into Whitehaven on 6 June 1934 as part of Navy Week. The vessel was commanded by Lt G.M. Sladen who was, at the time, an international rugby union player.

The South or West Pier was added to the harbour in 1838 after five years of difficult construction work. Although battered by some severe storms over the years, it has stood the test of time and is a credit to its builders. Here the *Clearway* is seen returning to harbour in 1989 after dumping its load of mud and gravel.

Until just three years ago this was the scene every time the tide receded from the harbour. During the Second World War, bombing targets for the RAF to practise on were made and repaired on the slipway. As late as 1968 the tracks for handling the targets were still in place. Today the harbour is under water permanently and the slip is the start of the C2C cycle route.

A barque rounds the Devil's Elbow as it makes its way out to sea and starts its homeward journey in 1904. This fine image is taken from one of Jimmy O'Neil's collection of postcards of Whitehaven.

A collier vessel being towed out to where it can take advantage of the wind, outside the protection of the piers. The vessel was then free to sail away to its ultimate destination, probably Belfast or Dublin. The fog warning device by the lighthouse was still very much part of the scene in 1900.

Whitehaven harbour must have been a welcome sight to mariners in the early part of the nineteenth

century and some of the magic has been well captured in this fine old painting of the time.

A couple of unnamed Whitehaven vessels lying off in 1880.

Over the past fifteen years or so the paddle steamer *Waverley* and its sister steamer *Balmoral* have taken passengers for a cruise down the Cumbrian coast or on a day trip to the Isle of Man. The *Waverley* is seen here in 1991 leaving for Douglas. These trips have proved to be very popular with Manx people now making the reverse journey.

Looking along the Old Quay towards the South Beach and the Wellington Inn, the dominant landmark is the Candlestick Chimney, once the ventilation shaft of the Wellington Pit. This now serves as a memorial to all those men and children who lost their lives in the pursuit of coal. While at one time the whole scene was hustle and bustle, by 1980 things were much quieter.

The true extent of the Red Flag Inn can be gauged from this photograph from 1904. Its location at the top of the cliffs overlooking the Wellington Pit is said to have inspired Jonathan Swift to write about the little people in *Gulliver's Travels*.

Two contrasting views of the Wellington Colliery from around 1900. The first is an artist's impression of the mighty pit with all the strength and power associated with the coal industry highly accentuated. The harbour is full of the kinds of activity generated by the production and export of coal. The second image is taken from a hand tinted photographic postcard produced by local printer W.H. Moss. Like Saltom Pit, Wellington was sunk just above the high water mark giving the mine owners two distinct advantages. Firstly it was not necessary to sink the shaft so deeply as was the case with other pits in the area and secondly high tides could be relied upon to wash the colliery waste out to sea and in doing so keep the spoil heaps to a constant level. The pit closed in 1932 but it was not until 1956 that the buildings were demolished and the slag used to build the spectators' terraces at the Recreation Ground.

During the many bitter miners' strikes and management lock-outs there was little to occupy the normally active workforce. Money was tight or non-existent so the simplest of games helped pass the time away. The front of the seamen's mission provided the backdrop for a serious game of marbles in 1910.

The Old Quay is the venue for another way to kill time – a game of cards. No doubt a few pennies would be wagered – giving the winner at least the price of a pint. This particular game must have been tense judging by the looks of concentration on the faces of Mr Cradduck and his mates.

The Seamen's Mission or Bethel, seen here in 1907, was first opened in 1824 and after a period of disuse reopened in 1869. The Bethel was very closely linked with the Congregational church on Scotch Street whose ministers and officers all took a hand in running the Bethel's affairs. In later years the building was used by the Whitehaven branch of the YWCA.

Every Whitsuntide and November a fair was held in Whitehaven, filling the whole of the West Strand and harbour side as far as the Duncan Square. Rides and roundabouts have changed quite a bit since the 1880s!

Five

Lowther Street
to Corkickle

Leaving the South Harbour by way of New Lowther Street, we continue our journey up one of the most attractive and busiest streets in the town. Originally designed to lead from the Castle to the harbour, it was intended that the street would be lined with large, well-designed, and handsome properties. These mansions were to be the town houses of the many wealthy merchants who had settled in the town and would give the visitor a feeling of Whitehaven's prosperity. St Nicholas' church was moved from the end of Chapel Street to its present location in the centre of Lowther Street in 1693. The street was also chosen to house the Granary, built by the Lowthers to ensure that there was always a good supply of grain at reasonable and consistent prices for the mine workers, at times of shortage or when the market price was too high. During the nineteenth century many of these fine buildings became banks or retail outlets, printing works or newspaper offices. The Carnegie Library was located in Catherine Street, just off Lowther Street, along with the Citadel of the Salvation Army. At the head of Lowther Street is the Castle, home of the Lowther family for more than 200 years. Continuing southwards we arrive at that part of Whitehaven known as Corkickle, the home of the town's southern railway station and the Tower Brewery.

New Lowther Street looking south from the harbour as it was in 1904, just three years before the Bethel was substantially altered, losing one storey in the process. Today the buildings to the left are all part of the offices of solicitors H.T. Gough and Co.

Built in 1709 by Anthony Borrowdale for a number of different clients, Nos 35 to 39 New Lowther Street had changed little even by 1965. Most of these properties are now part of W.H. Gough & Co.'s offices. Brandaw (electrical contractors) were founded by John Brannon and Bob 'Fizzer' Dawson, the Australian rugby league player who played for Whitehaven Rugby League Football Club.

Suttons Clock was a well known landmark on Lowther Street and Rideout and Bennett were popular ladies', gents' and children's outfitters. During the latter part of the eighteenth century the building was an inn called the Old Pack Horse.

Lowther Street was a busy place in 1901, with many well-known shops on either side of the road. Looking towards the harbour, those on the left are: No. 28, The Pack Horse Hotel; 29, John R. Foster, spirits merchant; 30, Henry T. Weld, draper; and 31, Robert Sutton, watchmaker. On the right are: No. 55, George Mitchell, tobacconist; 56, B. Taylor, hairdresser; 57, William Charnley, butcher; and 58, Thomas Bowman, grocer.

Several 'Bands of Hope' round the corner from King Street on their way to St Nicholas' church for Sunday morning church parade in 1901. Note Charnley the family butchers, also seen in the picture above. Bands of Hope were the forerunners of the Boys' Brigade, the Whitehaven branch of which was based, in later years, at the Christ Church Hall in Coach Road.

George Mitchell had moved his tobacconist's business to No. 56 Lowther Street by 1932 and had put on a fine display of pipes for National Pipe Week. This photograph was taken by another George Mitchell – George E. Mitchell whose studio was across the road at No. 29. Note the cost of twenty cigarettes for 1s!

H.T. Weld, cash drapers, moved from No. 1 King Street to 'The Louvre' (30 Lowther Street), before this photograph was taken in 1905. In later years the premises were occupied by Lucas and Cussons who were quality ladies' and gentlemen's tailors and outfitters. Salesman Frank Kitchen always served the customer with a smile and a friendly word, and he was also a keen youth worker at the Murray Boys' Club. Frank was a member of St Nicholas' church choir until the day the nave and sanctuary were completely destroyed by fire on 31 August 1971. Until that dreadful day the church was the principal Anglican place of worship and celebration in the town. The full majesty and beauty of the church is well captured in this fine drawing by Charles J. Ferguson.

Scout and Guide troops were often attached to churches and other youth or religious organizations. St Nicholas' church certainly did have both groups, which met at the church rooms in Scotch Street. This group was photographed in 1930 by George E. Mitchell – it would be nice to know for certain just who these delightful ladies were!

While this photograph of Lowther Street between Church Street and the harbour is not of the best quality, it is an important one and dates from around 1890. The property on the left, which is today called the Gear Box, was then a dwelling house of just two storeys with a double gable end. The image serves to show just how important old photographs can be in showing exactly how a place looked in days gone by.

The Oddfellows' Hall was a fine-looking building in 1901. The ground floor was occupied by a number of different businesses, including from the left: John Hindson Douglas, drapers; M.A. & W. Atkinson, ladies' outfitters; and the Misses Allinson, fancy goods.

By the 1960s the roof of the hall was unstable and considered unsafe. Occupying the shop premises then were Wandless chemists, and Parnaby furnishers. The top floor was used for many a function over the years. Who remembers Dick Barton's square dance band?

Located in Lowther Street in the 1920s, Whitehaven Building Society states 'House Purchase Made Easy'. The customer's car parked outside is a typical family car of the times – no heater, no radio, no windscreen washers and started by hand-cranking the engine!

The buildings on the right-hand side of Lowther Street were still in use as town houses in 1860. The large property on the corner of Queen Street was once a merchant's house which found later use as a bank. Today it is a restaurant and bar. Note the high railings which surround St Nicholas' church – these were removed during the Second World War for use in the production of much-needed steel.

Built in 1731, the Granary stood where the library and the Dunboyne Hall are located today. It is seen here shortly before demolition in 1949. The roof structure and the well-designed ventilation system are of interest. The Civic Hall car park now occupies the site and the Dunboyne Hall was opened on 17 October 1956 by the Mayor, Councillor George Hanlon JP.

The Carnegie Library in Catherine Street, named after its benefactor Andrew Carnegie, was opened in 1906 and continued to serve the local community in its original form until 1974, at which time it became part of the Cumbria County Library Service.

Whitehaven provided recruits for the 34th Regiment of Foot as long ago as 1702 when the Regiment was first raised. In October 1959 the 1st Battalion of the Border Regiment was amalgamated with the King's Own Royal Regiment to form the King's Own Royal Border Regiment. In September 1964 it was granted the Freedom of the Borough and soldiers celebrated with a march round town wearing uniforms from the regiment's past.

During the Second World War the 9th Battalion of the Border Regiment fought in Burma as part of General Orde Wingate's Chindit group. As part of the 1964 celebrations, this squad marched through Whitehaven in the uniform of the 9th Battalion.

Standing on the corner, opposite the library, was Whitehaven Motors, which traded until the property was demolished in 1964. They were part of the Stouts Garages Ltd group, motor engineers who prided themselves on being RAC and AA recommended and agents for Exide. The company's Roper Street premises handled the work of Whitehaven Motors after the garage was converted into an ICI petrol station by the new owner, Harry Graham.

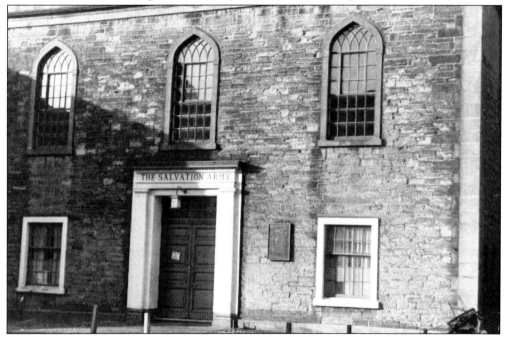

The Salvation Army came to Whitehaven in October 1885 under the guidance of Sarah Morton and Sarah Ann Hugill. At first, meetings were held in a room over a Tangier Street coffee shop but by 1937 the Army had moved into the Methodist Chapel in Catherine Street. Pictured in 1960, the crumbling old building was replaced by today's Citadel in October 1971.

Photographed by George E. Mitchell in 1928, these two officers of the Whitehaven company give some indication of the serenity and joy membership of the Salvation Army can bring. It would complete the picture to know who these ladies were.

The Salvation Army began with a series of 'Christian Revival Services' conducted by William Booth in London. In his addresses he used the phrase 'Salvation Army' – and the rest is history. In his later years William Booth visited Whitehaven, staying at Sorbie, the home of the McGowans.

Surrounded by a high wall, Whitehaven Castle dominated the scene at the head of Lowther Street in 1905. Sir John Lowther purchased The Flatt, as the property was then known, from Sir George Fletcher in 1675 and had it substantially altered to his own designs. The heir to the estate, Sir James Lowther, completely rebuilt the house in 1769, renaming it Whitehaven Castle.

Herbert W. Walker purchased the Castle and in 1923 presented it, along with sufficient funds to set up a hospital, to the people of Whitehaven. The NHS was formed in 1948 and Whitehaven hospital became part of the free state medical service and served the local community until a new building was opened at Hensingham in 1956. After this, the Castle continued to be used as a day-care centre for the elderly.

Bordering the Castle is an area of town known as Corkickle where sixty council houses were erected in 1921 on an estate called The Gardens. There were no proper scaffolding, dumper trucks or fork lifts in those days, when construction work was completed by hand. The Castle Saw Mills can be seen in the background.

The Whitehaven and Furness Junction Railway was incorporated on 21 April 1847 and required a tunnel to join Bransty and Corkickle stations. Constructed between 1850 and 1852, the tunnel was brick-built and single track. The train passing through the tunnel carried the key without which the signals and the points could not be operated and which the driver, as shown here in 1909, passed to a waiting official.

W. J. ARMSTRONG,

Brewer,

WHOLESALE WINE & SPIRIT MERCHANT,

AND

MINERAL WATER MANUFACTURER.

Telephone, Brewery: No. 16.   Telephone, Spirit Stores: No. 14.

Tower Brewery,

and

13 King Street, Whitehaven.

The Tower Brewery Company was started by the Peile family in 1771 and, despite a regular and considerable turnover of owners, the premises were operated as such until 1932. At that time William Jackson Armstrong was declared bankrupt and the brewery together with twenty fully licensed public houses, two beer houses and seventeen cottages were sold by public auction on 8 December 1932 at the Masonic Hall, Duke Street. The loss of the business together with that of Old Brewery in Irish Street left Whitehaven without a brewery.

Whitehaven Congregational church, c. 1920. The church was built between October 1872 and November 1874; it replaced an earlier building which was described as dark and draughty. The new church, built in concrete and faced with stone, was designed by Mr T.L. Banks and cost £10,000 to erect. Later, the congregation began to dwindle and in 1969 the church merged with the Presbyterian church in the Market Place. The building was sold and, after use as a DIY store, it was demolished and replaced by a new police station and magistrates' court.

Six

Scotch Street,
High Street
and Brackenthwaite

Originally, that part of Whitehaven lying to the north of Duke Street was called Brackenthwaite. The first property to be built in the area was Capt. Senhouse's house, erected in 1686/87 and now known as The Waverly Hotel. At that time Duke Street was the main entrance to the Castle or Flatt. Nevertheless, development of the street was already well underway and by 1705 the area between Queen Street and Scotch Street was built up. Six years later the whole of Brackenthwaite was under development and by 1750 all the present streets were in existence. St James' church was completed in 1753, to a plan by Carlisle Spedding, who was Lowther's mining agent. St James' National School was completed seventy years later. In this chapter our journey round town takes in many of the streets and buildings which formed part of that early Brackenthwaite.

John B. Walker was long established as a grocer and provision merchant by the time this photograph was made in 1885. He was also the licensee of the pub next door, the Three Tuns. The two parts of the tannery were connected by a covered bridge which can be seen at the top of the street.

Started by George Miller in 1765, the tannery eventually passed into the hands of the Walker family in 1858, with whom it remained until the closure of the works in 1958. In 1961 the derelict building was pulled down and the site cleared, making way for the Edinburgh-based car sales and service centre company, SMT.

Morning service is over and church is out; the congregation leaves St James' and makes its leisurely way along High Street in the summer of 1901. The group of girls are probably from the Girls' Orphan Home in Granby Place and the schoolboys were from the Piper's Marine School on High Street.

St James' church provides a fitting backdrop to this garden scene from 1920. Today the garden forms part of the grounds of St James' Infants' School, which was extended in 1961. The church clock was made by a local blacksmith and restored, together with other parts of the church, in 1886 at a cost of £866.

The General Associate Presbytery in Sanquhar granted a request for 'supply of sermon' to twenty-seven Scotsmen who were living in Whitehaven and as a result The Kirk was built on High Street in 1760. It is pictured in 1910, many years after the congregation of the Kirk was combined with that of the Presbyterian church in the Market Place. The Kirk was then in use as a Methodist Mission.

The Primitive Methodists using The Kirk as a mission were notable for the high proportion of their congregation who became lay preachers or entered the full-time ministry. During 1935 a number of the members of the mission attended the Cliff College and are seen here with their families.

Not a great deal is known about the observatory, the subject of this postcard in 1904. Situated at the top of Wellington Row and overlooking both the town and its approaches from the north, it was well positioned for a machine gun and military observation post. Some people believe it to have been an astronomical observatory, but its very mode of construction rules that out.

A spectacular view could be had in 1938, looking across to Bransty from the White Park. Evidence of coal mining was never far away in any general view of Whitehaven and the position of William and Henry pits is confirmed by the presence of the chimneys in the background. The former James Pit shaft was used as a ventilation shaft by other newer pits and is located to the right of the picture.

The name 'House of Correction Lane' was in local use until quite recently and refers to the northern end of Peter Street. Originally built in 1713, the house was converted into a jail a few years later. It was finally closed for business in 1858 and reverted to dwelling houses – Nos. 1 and 2 Peter Street as seen here in 1930. The properties were demolished in 1956 and the site was redeveloped for council flats.

This section of Queen Street contained some of the few properties spared the attentions of the bulldozer in 1956. Whilst virtually all around fell and was replaced by council flats, the Jolly Sailor was preserved but without its licence to sell wines, ales and spirits. Although the frontage was kept, the inside of the building was fully modernized.

Just a few yards away from the Jolly Sailor stood the Commercial Hotel which at one time was also the site of the Queen Street Brewery. This property was also preserved and converted into sheltered accommodation for the handicapped. In the late 1960s wholesale demolition of the town centre was stopped when it was finally realized just how much of the town's history and heritage was being destroyed.

George W. Mitchell photographed these two happy chaps and their somewhat battered and bent Armstrong-Siddley car in 1930. Whether the pen is poised above a route map or an estimate for repairs is anybody's guess! For the fashion minded, the gentlemen are wearing long leather coats and white spats, no doubt essential items of apparel for a drive in the country.

One of Whitehaven's earliest car sales rooms and garages was that of the Taylor family on Duke Street – The Central Garage. Joe Taylor also operated one of the two taxi services then in town from the family's cycle shop further down the street. Seen here in 1960 the garage was demolished, together with many dwelling houses around about it, making way for new council flats. Not far from the garage, at Nos 26 and 27 Duke Street, were Mounsey's fried fish and chip shop and newsagent and tobacconist, E.M. Rae. Both of these popular businesses survive today although under different ownership. Next door to Mounsey's is the Sal Madge public house, which has recently undergone one of its several transmutations and periodic alterations. It was originally called the Cow, later the Brown Cow, then the Sun and until recently was the Dolphin. Ales, wines and spirits have been sold on the site for almost 300 years.

This early photograph of Duke Street in around 1880 gives an indication of what life was like without the motor vehicle. At No. 103 William Sim snipped away at his customers' hair for more than 40 years. Before Mr. Sim the job had been carried out by Robert Hume and after Sim had retired, John Reid continued trimming and shaving until 1913. Richard Bell then took up the scissors for several more years.

An early motor vehicle threads its way through groups of unconcerned pedestrians on Duke Street in 1910. Although the scene is similar to the previous photograph the tradespeople have changed and these include the following, from left to right: the Central Hotel; Banks & Co., tailors; Taylor & Wilkinson, tailors; William Wilkinson, saddlers; the Globe Hotel; the Wheatsheaf Hotel; the Ship Inn; William Bell, marine stores; Louis Leefson, hairdresser; Florence Tuley, draper; the Cleator Moor Co-op; John Davis, grocer; Anna Nicholson, confectioner; Peter Danzie, tobacconist; Joseph Williams, fancy draper; Thomas Cinnamon, tobacconist; Thomas Roe, provisions merchant; Edward Kennaugh, plumber; and the Graves Bros, pawnbrokers.

A stroll up Duke Street in the 1920s would take one past a good many different businesses including, starting from the harbour: the Cleator Moor Co-op, complete with horse-drawn delivery van; John Whittle, furniture; R.H. Thorpe, ironmonger; Peter Danzie; Joe Williams; Thomas Cinnamon; the Whitehaven Steam Laundry; Thomas Roe; Edward Kennaugh; Graves Bros; Joseph Williamson, butcher; Thomas Vickers, greengrocer; Thomas Ashbridge, butcher; Robert McGowan, pork butcher; J. McBain, fishmonger; Thomas E. Bell, grocer; Robert Woodnorth, painter; the Sun Inn; Jacob Dixon, draper; Maxwell Mounsey, fried fish merchant; Jane Richardson, pastry cook; Edna and Margaret Nancarrow, ladies' hairdressers; Charles McGuiness, grocer; the Central Garage; and The Ship Inn.

The Davis family ran the grocers and cocoa rooms at No. 6 Duke Street for many years. Next door in 1904 was William's Restaurant and the Brides Café. Their Tangier Street neighbour was C.W. Atkinson, pork butcher and bacon curer, and several years later the premises became the Rubber Shop.

Seven

King Street, The Market Place and Howgill Street

Although Lowther Street was intended to be the main street in the town, most people, if asked, would give that honour to King Street which has been described as 'the Golden Mile'. In reality it is barely a quarter of a mile long but, in its day, it was the business centre of the town and had several dozens of shops in which to spend one's money; indeed anybody that was anybody had his shop or head office on the street. Today its image as the 'golden mile' is more than a little dulled – patterns of trade have changed and the family businesses all but gone – but nevertheless it remains the principal street for general shopping. The southern end of King Street runs into the Market Place where there are still two open markets each week. At one time markets were held every Tuesday, Thursday and Saturday, coinciding with the livestock auction markets, but today the livestock business has gone and only the latter two market days remain to remind us of busy times now past. Just a short stroll away is Howgill Street, once home of the local Scientific Society, the Infirmary and the Trinity School. In this chapter we look at these streets before returning to the harbour side via Trinity church, the Theatre Royal and Roper Street.

Even in 1905, 'Top' King Street was a busy place, certainly busier than today. From an architectural standpoint almost all of the shops at ground floor level have been radically altered but most of the upper frontages remain undisturbed and are still attractive to the student of architecture. Note the granite set stones used, almost exclusively, for the construction of surface water drains.

Top King Street remained busy and in 1910 presents an active picture, but at the top of the street William's restaurant has given way to confectioner Emma Hartley. The Black Lion Hotel, one of the town's more important establishments, was a popular place for travellers to stay and just a little further up the street Wallace Bros offered 'This Season's Models, Boots and Shoes'. Other traders on the Street included, from left to right: W. Holloway, toys etc.; W. Strathern, plumber; the Black Lion; H. Adair, tailor; J. Kitchen, glass and china; A. Kerr, milliner; W. Bewley, grocer; Stead and Simpson, shoes; I. Martin, ladies' outfitters; W. Anderson, draper; the Prince Albert Vaults; W. Ainsworth, draper; Wallace Bros, boots and shoes; W.H. Smith, newsagents; Charles Bie, shoemaker; and the Globe Hotel.

Low King Street has always been the busier of the two and there were many and varied ways to spend your cash. One such place was the Maypole Dairy at No. 40 which was to trade for half a century or more before the site was swallowed up by an expanding Woolworths in the 1960s. Prices in 1905 were rather different than those of today: margarine cost 4d to 6d per pound and tea 8d per pound. For those who preferred it, butter could be had at 1s 1d a pound. All nice and cheap – but when we consider the wages which in those days were measured in shillings and not pounds, things were not quite so rosy! Just a little further up the street, in 1960, stood Whitehaven's first supermarket; the Home & Colonial Store; Freeman, Hardy and Willis; Curry's; New Modes and Greenwood the gents' outfitters.

A look up King Street in 1904, from the entrance to the Shambles or Low Meat Market, gives some indication of the melange of trades carried out on the street at that particular time. These are, from left to right: John Gray & Co., boot-makers; Catherine Skinner, confectioner; James Brown, cabinet maker; S.L. Jones, basket maker; Lipton Ltd, grocers; John Nevison, hatter; The Alliance Boot Co.; J.T. Lowery, shoe maker; James Lowery, draper; J.W. Fisher, eating house; Thomas Browne, draper; Hannah and Slade, drapers; Jeremiah Gunson, draper; J. McIlwraith, brush maker; Wilson & Kitchen, chemists; W.H. Telford, watch maker; the Albion Hotel; the Cash Clothing Co.; J Stalker, grocer; C.T. Gordon, ironmonger; the Singer Sewing Machine Co.; J. Tyson and Sons, drapers; and the Shambles Meat Market.

The Market Place has always had a touch of animation about it and the summer of 1905 was no exception. Looking from the corner of Queen Street, formerly Tickell Lane, towards the new Market Hall we can see the Anchor Vaults; the Bird in the Hand Inn; Thomas Wison, butcher; Guselli and Gazzi, café proprietors; Samuel Stewart, clothes dealer; S. Simpson, greengrocer; the Queen Arms Inn; and John Hunter, hairdresser.

Market Place shoppers had no motor traffic to contend with in 1905, as goods were brought in either by horse and cart or by hand cart or barrow. Instead of the covered market stall of today goods were sold directly from the cart. The outward appearance of the shops on the right has changed little in the 100 years or so since this photograph was taken.

John Sibson's fruit and vegetable stall was always popular with shoppers. So successful was Mr Sibson that he was able to open up a couple of shops in the Market Place, selling green groceries alongside garden plants and sundries. Seen here in 1960, wearing his trademark Fedora hat, John serves his customers with a smile and a touch of banter. On the extreme left of the picture is his son Don who followed his father in the business until it closed in 1998.

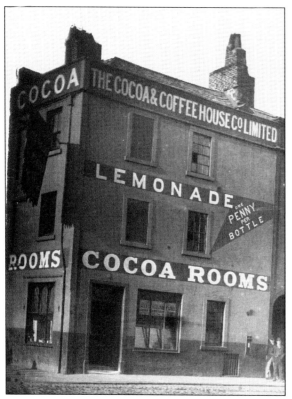

Both J. & J. Braithwaite and the Cocoa and Coffee House Co. were thriving concerns in 1901. Braithwaites described themselves as ironmongers and ships' chandlers, though just what a ship's captain would do with an agricultural sickle or a 'posser' remains a mystery! Braithwaites sold just about everything the householder could possibly require from barbed wire to fancy oil lamps. Apart from the obligatory cocoa or coffee, the Cocoa Rooms sold lemonade at 1d per bottle and offered ginger ale and juice and limes to the thirsty customer. Note the post box, not twenty yards away from the Market Place post office. The archway which separated the two businesses led into Gale Back Lane and in later years the Cocoa House became Walter Wilsons and Braithwaites changed into T.W. Dixon, the wet fish merchants.

A Presbyterian church has stood in Whitehaven Market Place since 1695, at which time Elisha Gale, Henry Palmer, William Atkinson, William Feryes and John Shepherd were granted a parcel of land and were empowered to build a chapel on the site. The church was renovated in 1856/57 at a cost of £800 and was totally rebuilt in 1905, not long after this photograph was taken, by Whytes of Jamaica Street, Glasgow. While the church looked after the soul, the body was mended at the Infirmary located just around the corner in Howgill Street. In 1926, Mr James Bellman was commissioned to produce photographs of the Infirmary before it ceased operating and moved to its new location in the Castle. The fine old building was once the home of Thomas Hartley, a prominent merchant in the town; it later become the Trinity National School and in the war years acted as an annexe for Whitehaven County Secondary School. Afterwards it became a shirt factoy for Coles of Knightsbridge

The Infirmary received its first patients on 1 May 1830, under the care of the first of a long line of matrons – Mrs Stock. She was followed by Mrs Jane Holiday in 1832 and she held the post for the next thirty-three years! These south-facing balconies were erected in 1897 so that patients could feel the benefit of 'good fresh air and enjoy the sun'.

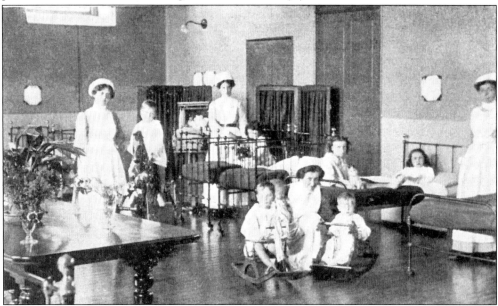

As part of his 1926 commission, James Bellman captured this image of the children's ward which was run by a sister and three nurses. Following the opening of the Infirmary in 1830, two further wards were opened in 1857, built at the expense of Baroness de Sternberg. In her will the Baroness provided for a further two wards and she left a Samaritan fund to the hospital.

The Trinity National School was established in Howgill Street in 1852, before moving to the old infirmary building in 1933. The school metalwork shop stood in the low building which now houses Jackson's timber yard. The school was proud of these new facilities, pictured here in a photograph by George W. Mitchell on the day they were opened in 1933. Every pupil had his own bench space and a good vice with which to work.

Trinity School encouraged their boys to make the most of themselves in every possible way. Sporting prowess was one way of giving the boys the confidence they would need in their adult life. The school team was particularly successful and in 1940 won both the County Shield and the Moss Shield. Pictured with their teacher L. Fitzsimmons are, from left to right, back row: T. Sayles, Isaac Douglas, R. Oldfield. Middle row: W. McQuire, R. Lewis, R. Graham, Tommy Haddows, E. Houston. Front row: R. Orr, W. Scurr, Jackie Sewell, L. Vaughan, A. Messenger.

Photographed for its opening day in 1901, the new cricket pavilion was erected that same year at the Play Ground. Whitehaven played in the North Lancashire League and were champions on several occasions. Many players of international standing played as the Saturday professional, including Bill Lawton (Lancashire and England), Greg Matthews (Australia) and, in 1955/56, New South Wales batsmen Nev Emery and Dick Beard, who took the league by storm.

The Play Ground was also home to the town's Bowls and Tennis Clubs. It is interesting to see that at this 1901 bowls tournament the white jack is almost as big as the bowls themselves! Although the Whitehaven bowlers were successful for many years, membership of the club dwindled and the greens suffered. By the 1960s bowling at the Play Ground had ceased.

Roper Street, one of Whitehaven's older thoroughfares, was headed by Trinity church, which was erected in 1714/15 at a cost of £2,075, and consecrated by the Bishop of Chester on 2 October 1715. Dwindling congregations led to a merger with Christ Church, Preston Street, in 1935. Seen here in 1949, Trinity church was demolished on the grounds of public safety. Just a few yards down the street the Theatre Royal opened for business in 1769 and it remained a going concern until the 1930s despite undergoing several re-constructions, the last occurring in 1909. Whitehaven audiences were finicky and in 1922 even the great Sir Donald Wolfit was given the 'bird'! The theatre, seen here in 1960 prior to demolition, made way for a new printing line for the *Whitehaven News*.

Between the two world wars people tended to entertain themselves or were members of an amateur operatic society, concert party or theatre group. Many of these amateur entertainers put on their shows and pantomimes at Whitehaven's theatres and concert rooms and although we may never know precisely what George W. Mitchell photographed here in 1929, the pictures are a good example of the type of home-grown entertainment available in the town. The chorus line might be Captain Hook's pirate crew in *Peter Pan*, while the other image is most probably a formal portrait of one of the carnival queens. For now these images must remain a mystery unless, of course, a reader knows otherwise.

Eight

Shipbuilding and the North Harbour

Over the years the North Harbour took on a greater level of importance, initially as the location of the shipbuilding industry and later, as the direct result of the opening of the Queens Dock, as a commercial base for imported goods and the export of coal. The merchants of the town had pressed for a wet dock for well over a century and always without any real hope of success, because the Lowther family were initially unwilling to support a project which would be of benefit only to a limited number of people. They only agreed to its construction when growing coal exports required the use of bigger ships. The wet dock was built between 1872 and 1876; however, it was too small and came much too late in the development of the harbour to prevent the loss of Whitehaven's North American and Caribbean trade to the likes of Glasgow and Liverpool. The tobacco trade had already suffered a near mortal blow when England lost the American War of Independence. In this chapter we examine the variety of the day-to-day harbour business and the last days of the shipyards. Today the whole of the harbour has been renovated for the new business of the day – recreation and tourism.

The harbour of the 1860s was a busy place, despite the fact that the wet dock had not yet been constructed. Shipbuilding was a major player in the local economy and after coal mining it was the chief employer in the town. The recently completed tunnel and new Bransty railway station all added to the slow and irreversible demise of the business of the harbour.

The SS *Downshire* was a regular visitor to Whitehaven harbour in the early twentieth century. This postcard tells us a little about her end – sunk by a German submarine on Saturday 20 February 1917.

Typical of a working day in the harbour of 1904, this scene shows a sailing brig being towed out to where its sails can find sufficient wind for the voyage to foreign parts. Meanwhile the dredger, attended by its barges, works away clearing the channel for the bigger boats which used the harbour. Further out a couple fishing smacks catch the breeze and head for the fishing grounds.

In 1910 a group of volunteers with the Rocket Brigade were presented with long service (twenty-five years) medals at a ceremony at the Grand Hotel. The Rocket Brigade was formed in 1849, becoming part of the Coastguard in 1864. Those receiving their medals by order of King George V were: Capt. Wilson, Lt McGill, Messrs J. Devine, J. Connor and L. Wilson.

The Whitehaven lifeboat crew pose in front of their boat, the *Elizabeth Leicester II* in 1910 together with their patron, the Earl of Lonsdale. The lifeboat station had been manned by volunteers since 1804 and continued to be so until 1925 when the *Elizabeth* was taken out of service and never replaced. Whitehaven's needs were met by the Workington lifeboat from that time forward.

On Tuesday 6 June 1934, the battle cruiser HMS *Iron Duke* paid an official visit to Whitehaven as part of Navy Week. The vessel was Admiral Jellicoe's flagship at the Battle of Jutland in 1916. Now flying the flag of Rear-Admiral F.N. Laurence DSO, the ship was commanded by Captain H.C. Allen and both officers and crew took part in many sporting events as well as dances and concerts laid on by the townsfolk.

On the first day of the visit the mayor, Alderman W Stephenson, paid an official visit to the ship. He was accompanied by T.C. Bone (Town Clerk), Revd T.A. Agius (Mayor's Chaplain), Mr W. Nunn MP, Lt-Col. G. Dixon (deputy chairman of Whitehaven magistrates), Mr O.F. Ormrod, (magistrates' clerk), and the Chief Constable of Cumberland, Once on board they were greeted by Rear-Admiral Laurence, Paymaster Lt-Cmdr C.W. Brockman; Lt-Cmdr J.D. Crossman and other ship's officers.

Backing up the visit of HMS *Iron Duke*, one of His Majesty's submarines, *H50*, also paid a visit to Whitehaven. Unlike the battle cruiser, *H50* was able to enter the harbour and tied up in the Queen's Dock on 6 June 1934. Wellington Pit, in the background, had closed in the previous year, which allowed the Navy to do a spot of recruiting.

Bound for Casablanca to pick up a load of phosphate rock, the *Marchon Venturer* leaves harbour in 1965. The silos were built and owned by Marchon and were used for the buffer storage of the rock. The company had three ships, all built in the North East especially for the Casablanca run with the latest, the *Venturer*, launched at Clelland's yard in Wallsend in February 1962.

A well-packed steamer cruises past the William and Henry Pits and the Lonsdale Ironworks, c. 1900. Flying a good set of nautical flags, the vessel looks a fine sight and may have been a regular visitor to Whitehaven.

The paddle tug *Florence* was one of several hired by the harbour commissioners from Dublin to do the duties which were once the province of their own vessel, the *Prince of Wales*. During the 1920s she could often by seen lying just outside the Queen's Dock waiting to give assistance to any larger vessel which may have needed a pull, push or tow around the Devil's Elbow.

The Maryport-based steam paddle tug *Senhouse* leaves Whitehaven, sailing close to the North Pier in 1894. The photograph gives a good indication of the extent of the Lonsdale Ironworks along the North Shore between William Pit and Redness Point. Note the three slag banks of which only one now remains: it is known locally as Whitey Rock, even though it is neither white nor a rock!

George Nelson painted the SS *Cumbria* entering harbour in 1904. The painting confirms the structure of the ironwork on the top of the North Light, which one day may be restored as part of today's ongoing harbour improvement scheme.

This unusual photograph of the coal-loading facilities at the Queen's Dock was taken sometime between 1890 and 1900. It gives some idea of the many rail tracks which ran around the harbour at that time.

This view along the tracks in the opposite direction from the previous photograph adds quite a bit to our knowledge of the harbour at that time. Despite the abundance of rails, a sizeable proportion of the goods were taken from and delivered to the ships in the harbour by horse and cart. Completing the picture the Grand Hotel raises high above a busy, if somewhat murky scene.

In order to facilitate the building of the Queen's Dock in 1872, part of the North Wall together with the wooden jetty which ran parallel to it, had to be removed and a new watertight wall built in their stead. In addition the plans called for the Bulwark to be physically moved 20 yards to the left. Although the exact date of this photograph is not known, it must have be taken prior to the removal of the jetty in 1872.

The Dock Offices, seen here in 1895, were built in 1876. After sustaining severe damage in a storm in 1894, they were repaired and the clock tower was increased in height. Serious subsidence was discovered in the foundations of the building in 1956 leading to its demolition.

For the best part of 250 years Whitehaven Harbour was home to thousands of great sailing vessels trading with all parts of the globe but especially with the Baltic States, North America and the West Indies. The biggest ship to be built and fitted out at Whitehaven was the *Alice A. Leigh*, launched in October 1889. She weighed 2,929 tons and is seen here in 1890, before her maiden voyage, when the *Alice* attracted plenty of interest.

A mighty four-masted vessel sets sail for distant parts of the world, *c.* 1880. What she was called and where she was bound must remain her secret, but there is no denying the fact that she makes a fine picture as she heads out into the Irish Sea.

St George Henry Lowther became the 4th Earl of Lonsdale at the tender age of twenty and he found the time to attend just one meeting of the town and harbour trustees, on 22 June 1881. After the meeting he entertained the trustees to dinner on board his yacht *Northumbria* while it was moored in the Queen's Dock.

Berthed alongside that same stretch of harbour wall in the 1950s, the *Steinmark* of Bergen, Norway, was a fairly regular visitor to Whitehaven. Quaker Oats Ltd had just taken over the Pattinson family's Beacon Mills in 1949, which then employed some 130 people. The mill eventually closed and was demolished in 1972 after which Donnan's fish processing factory occupied the site.

Shipbuilding in Whitehaven began in the seventeenth century with the likes of Thomas Sibson (1686-1775), Benjamin Hadwin (1700-1790), and Joseph White (1714-1766) among the earliest builders. The yards were spread along the north shore from Duke Street to Redness Point. Stormy seas could not have made the shipbuilder's life an easy one in those early days before the protective clothing we are used to today.

In 1861 the *Tenasserim* was photographed as she was under construction in T. & J. Brocklebank's busy yard along side the old North Wall. The vessel measured 195ft in length with a beam of 35ft. When registered she had a draught of 22ft and weighed 1,002 tons. Sadly Brocklebank ceased to trade in Whitehaven in 1865, moving to Liverpool where the business later became part of the Cunard Line.

At 2,929 tons, the *Alice A. Leigh* was to be the largest vessel ever built at Whitehaven. Constructed by the Whitehaven Shipbuilding Co. No. 2, the *Alice* was launched in 1889 and was the second last ship to come out the Whitehaven yards, all of which were permanently closed by 1891. Tidal conditions made it impossible to launch the much larger vessels then required by the nation's merchant traders. In a brave attempt to stave off the inevitable, T. & J. Brocklebank took the bold decision to build all of their vessels from iron, with the first ship coming off the stocks in 1863. Just two years later Brocklebank and Co. had completed their move to Liverpool.

Well over 1,000 ships are known to have be built in the Whitehaven yards and of these most were collier brigs sized between 50 and 250 tons burthen. Collier vessels were built with flat bottoms and with double skinned hulls, a necessity for vessels which would spend a long time sitting on the mud of Whitehaven harbour while fully laden with coals. The *Unity* was one such vessel.

Towards the end of their life, the Whitehaven yards were building ever bigger ships, some of which were made from iron. The *Dunboyne* was one of the last ships to built by the Whitehaven Shipbuilding Co. No. 2 and weighed 1,355 tons when launched on 28 February 1888. Now called the *A.F. Chapman*, the vessel is still afloat in Stockholm harbour where she serves as a youth hostel.

Nine

Tangier Street and Local Transport

Situated on the west coast of Cumbria, it is not surprising that for a good many years the sea should have been a major player in the transportation of the people of Whitehaven and of their goods and materials. Indeed right up to the time of the First World War there were regular sailings to Dublin, Glasgow and Liverpool, with other vessels occasionally going to Bristol and London. It was even possible to sail to Port Carlisle and to travel onwards to the city by barge, coach or railway. After the railway came to Whitehaven in 1847, journeying to other parts of Britain could be made by train in greater comfort and style than had previously been the case. The railway was also a much quicker mode of travel and this factor alone brought about the inevitable demise of all the other forms of transport then in use. Such was the success of the train that Whitehaven needed two railway terminals to handle the number of travellers who wished to use the railway. Following the formation of the Whitehaven and Furness Junction Railway Co. Ltd in 1849, the two stations were joined by a mile long tunnel. There was a third station in the town, located in Preston Street and used for the transportation of goods; further distribution about the town was by means of the horse and cart, of which the railway had several. Even the railway was forced to take a back seat when the omnibus and motor car can along. In this chapter we pause for breath on our journey and take a look at local transport over the past hundred years or so.

This general view of Whitehaven dates from 1904 and embraces Bransty station and the harbour. Dominating the right of the photograph is the newly built Beacon Flour Mills, which transported all their requirements of grain by sea for the whole life span of the mill.

Whitehaven in 1856 was a very different place from today, with the Lonsdale Hotel (later the Grand) still under construction. Between the hotel and the sea the shipyards were always busy and along side the North Wall, at the specially constructed wooden jetty, a number of vessels loaded iron ore while the Queen's Dock was still little more than a dream.

This postcard from 1904 says it all! Just look at the queues waiting to join the mail boat *Tynwald*, which sailed daily to the Isle of Man from the North Wall. Naturally sea transportation was the only way to move anybody or anything between the island and the mainland and at that time Whitehaven was the port of choice but, regrettably, that is not the case today.

Travellers needed somewhere to rest after a long journey and with the coming of the railways the Lonsdale Hotel was built near the railway station for their accommodation. Known later as the Grand Hotel, the building found use as the offices of the Whitehaven and Furness Junction Railway. The hotel eventually reverted to its proper business and, as here in 1905, was the scene of many a great festival.

The Grand hotel served as the starting point for the annual Lifeboat Parade which was always well supported. Safety at sea was of paramount importance to the seafaring folk of Whitehaven. As on many other occasions, in 1910, the lifeboat *Elizabeth Leicester II* started its fund raising journey round the streets of the town.

The Sunny Hill Carnival (a forerunner of the present Whitehaven Carnival) fared little better with the summer weather of 1920 than many others have since. In spite of the heavy rains, spectators turned out in their thousands to give support to the carnival as it wended its way from the Grand Hotel down Tangier Street.

Tangier Street in 1964 was a different proposition, with T.B. Hodgson Ltd being the first of the town's ironmongers to end their long association with the retail of electrical and engineering sundries and to concentrate on household wares under the new name of Homeflair. The Blue Bell Inn (with clock) is now an Indian restaurant whilst the old Co-op building has been subdivided into several small shop units.

Until the late 1920s anyone entering or leaving Whitehaven from the north had to pass under Bransty Arch. Originally built to carry coal wagons from the Whingill Colliery to the harbour, the arch fell into disuse and disrepair. Later it was considered a traffic hazard and despite a 3,000 signature petition to the contrary, the local council ordered it to be demolished on 10 March 1927.

William Brown & Sons, steam dyers and cleaners, was a thriving business in 1905. However, when Harry Meagean started the Cumberland Motor Services Co. Ltd in the years immediately following the First World War, with six ex-Army double-decker buses, a bus station was soon on the cards and William Brown's works gave way to this new venture.

The regular bus services quickly became very popular all around the county with services connecting Whitehaven to Egremont, Cleator Moor, Frizington, Workington, Keswick, Maryport, Carlisle, Penrith and even to Millom in the south. A suitably attired driver and his conductor pose, in 1925, by their unheated vehicle.

In addition to regular bus services, the mystery tour or day trip became very popular and in those early days (1920) one needed to be a hardy soul to take a trip in an open-top charabanc fitted with solid tyres.

Although their headquarters were at Whitehaven, The Cumberland Motor Services Co. Ltd quickly built other bus stations at Workington, Keswick, Carlisle, Silloth and Maryport. By 1941 the company had a fleet of 178 vehicles although in the late 1920s, when this photograph was taken, that number was somewhat lower. Following deregulation the company was eventually taken over by Stagecoach.

Cumberland Motor Services built repair shops and garages along side and at the back of Whitehaven bus station with an entry on Wellington Row. There are a couple of double-decker buses just visible inside this back door where, in 1950, a group of council dustmen await the return of the ash cart from the refuse dump at the Hensingham quarries.

The growth of motor transport brought with it a host of small and large garages and car dealerships. Myers and Bowman Ltd were one such group and at one time held the agencies for Hillman and Humber cars. Not content with that, Bill Myers built himself an aeroplane in the 1930s. *The Flying Flea* together with Bill himself were always popular visitors to the area's carnivals and shows.

The railway first came to Whitehaven from Harrington on 19 March 1847. This was the final section of the Whitehaven Junction Railway and the line was engineered by no less a personage than George Stephenson, the builder of the *Rocket* and the world's first railway between Stockton and Darlington. This early (1860) photograph of the original Bransty terminus gives some indication of just how popular the railway used to be!

Following on from the merger agreement in 1849 between the Whitehaven Junction Railway and the Furness Junction Railway, the stations at Corkickle and Bransty were connected by a long tunnel. At much the same time Bransty station was completely rebuilt. Seen here in 1970, it remained unchanged until replaced by today's modern ticket office.

Bransty station was a great building, having first and third class, and ladies' waiting rooms; a refreshment room and bar; a magazine and book stall; parcel and postal facilities; and three platforms. The book stall, seen here in 1925, remained in continuous use until the 1960s, selling everything the traveller could possibly require for his or her journey.

Travel in the age of steam was nothing if not exciting, with the smell of smoke, the hiss of steam and the dirt in the eye of the unwary traveller who was foolish enough to stick his head out of the window. Nevertheless a journey by train was a tolerable one, even if it was only as far as Carlisle – the ultimate destination of this train leaving Bransty station's No. 1 platform in 1938.

The LMS Railway was only too pleased to arrange a train trip or tour in the years between the two world wars. One such tour was around the many branch lines that criss-crossed West Cumberland, most of which had originally been built for moving coal and iron ore from mine to end user. Another trip was this, arranged in 1937, which hauled a full load of passengers out into the countryside around Whitehaven.

Ten

Parton and Lowca

About a mile north of Whitehaven, the village of Parton lies below the old Roman fort or station on the rocky heights of Moresby. Until the great storm of 1795, which destroyed the pier and harbour, Parton was a serious rival to Whitehaven for the coal export trade to Ireland. A good many of the working inhabitants of the village found employment at the coal mines which surrounded the area, or they were engaged in fishing for a livelihood. In later years the Parton and Harrington Brewery, the Parton Tannery and the Lowca Engine Works added to the list of potential employers for the villagers. In this final chapter we complete our journey from south to north and take a brief look at the life and times of the village over the past 100 years or so.

Looking northward from Briscoe Mount this postcard from the 1920s celebrates the building of Whitehaven's new loop road which fills the foreground as it swings from left to right. The new road effectively bypasses the old Toll House on the left. The turn to Parton is just past the end of Briscoe Crescent, whilst in the background several coal mines, the Tar Plant and the Lowca Engine Works churn out plenty of smoke.

Parton can also be approached by the railway which swings round the bay as it heads for the station in the middle of the village. Here in 1905 a train can be seen passing the brewery and the tannery which were both still in full production. The Parton and Harrington Brewery Company supplied two or three dozen pubs in West Cumberland, before the failure of the joint venture with Jennings Bros led to the closure of the brewery in 1923.

Parton Brewery workers in 1910, posing among the barrels in happier times before a disastrous 'working arrangement' with Jennings Bros of Cockermouth. The arrangement called for the cessation of brewing at Parton with Jennings supplying all of the Parton Brewery's tied pubs.

This photograph of the Williamson School rugby union team is unfortunately undated. The team is seen here along with the schoolmaster and a board containing just fifteen medals – one for each player, as there were of course no substitutes in those days.

Parton was large enough to boast several businesses of its own and at the time this image was made in 1901, Bulmer's trade directory listed no fewer than thirty-three separate traders in the village. John Litt, grocer and postmaster, was one of them, having converted his private dwelling house into a shop in 1890.

Seated outside Brewery House in 1895, the members of the first Parton town council make an imposing group of gentlemen. They include: William Carmichael (chairman), J.S. Peile, J. Dalzell, W. Brown, M. White, F.W. Vendel, T.G. Greener, R. Franks, J. Phillipson, J.T. Spencer, S. Davies, A. Fletcher, W. Lace.

A snowy day in 1900 highlights the shape and position of St Bridget's church and Moresby Hall high on the hill above Parton. The church replaced a much older building in 1822 and stands on the site of a Roman signal station with the Gothic arch of the old church still standing in the grounds. Moresby Hall was the family home of the Fletchers of Moresby, important mine owners and serious rivals to the Lowther family.

This postcard from 1901 gives a good idea of the extent of the Lowca Engineering Works which were founded in 1800 by Adam Heslop together with his brothers Crosley and Thomas. While working in Shropshire during 1790, Adam Heslop patented the steam engine and when he returned to Lowca it was with the express intention of building these famous steam engines for use in the local coal pits.

Attached to the nearby coal mines at Lowca was the Tar Plant were coal was used to make coke and gas. Tar was the inevitable by-product and at the tar works it was refined to give a whole variety of chemical products, including benzole. In 1920 some of the benzene plant workmen pose with a motorcycle of the time, and one which, perhaps, ran on the plant's product. The third from the right on the back row is Bill Spedding and at the far right is Dick Railton. At the far right on the front row is Dick Steel.

Foundry Road, Parton in 1920 was so named because it led straight to the engineering works and onwards to the coal mines and the tar plant at Lowca. A good many of the men of Parton earned their pay at one or other of these establishments. Today all the coal mines, the tar plant and the engineering works have all long ceased production with little remaining to say that they ever existed.

The Beach House at Parton stood bravely against all that the stormy seas could throw at it for a great many years. Owned by Isaac Dickinson in 1901 it finally succumbed to the constant pounding of the waves of the Irish Sea some years ago.